P9-CQN-079

EYEWITNESS TO HISTORY

SITTING BULL

in his own words

Gareth Stevens
PUBLISHING

By Julia McDonnell

Please visit our website, www.garethstevens.com. For a free color catalog of all our high-quality books, call toll free 1-800-542-2595 or fax 1-877-542-2596.

Library of Congress Cataloging-in-Publication Data

McDonnell, Julia.
Sitting Bull in his own words / by Julia McDonnell.
p. cm. — (Eyewitness to history)
Includes index.
ISBN 978-1-4824-1283-3 (pbk.)
ISBN 978-1-4824-1223-9 (6-pack)
ISBN 978-1-4824-1482-0 (library binding)
1. Sitting Bull, — 1831-1890 — Juvenile literature. 2. Dakota Indians — Kings and rulers — Biography — Juvenile literature. 3. Hunkpapa Indians — Kings and rulers — Biography — Juvenile literature. I. McDonnell, Julia, 1979 -. II. Title.
E99.D1 M38 2015
978.004—d23

First Edition

Published in 2015 by
Gareth Stevens Publishing
111 East 14th Street, Suite 349
New York, NY 10003

Copyright © 2015 Gareth Stevens Publishing

Designer: Katelyn E. Reynolds
Editor: Therese Shea

Photo credits: Cover, pp. 1 (Sitting Bull), 23 Universal History Archive/Getty Images; cover, pp. 1 (background illustration), 27 MPI/Getty Images; cover, p. 1 (logo quill icon) Seamartini Graphics Media/Shutterstock.com; cover, p. 1 (logo stamp) YashaTen/Shutterstock.com; cover, p. 1 (color grunge frame) DmitryPrudnichenko/Shutterstock.com; cover, pp. 1–32 (paper background) Nella/Shutterstock.com; cover, pp. 1–32 (decorative elements) Ozerina Anna/Shutterstock.com; pp. 1–32 (wood texture) Reinhold Leitner/Shutterstock.com; pp. 1–32 (open book background) Elena Schweitzer/Shutterstock.com; pp. 1–32 (bookmark) Robert Adrian Hillman/Shutterstock.com; p. 4 Hulton Archive/Getty Images; p. 4 (signature) McSush/Wikipedia.com; pp. 5, 20 De Agostini Picture Library/Getty Images; p. 7 Marilyn Angel Wynn/Nativestock/Getty Images; p. 8 W. H. Childs/Wikipedia.com; p. 9 Kmusser/Wikipedia.com; pp. 10–11 Everett Collection/Shutterstock.com; pp. 12–13, 21 U.S. National Archives and Records Administration/Wikipedia.com; p. 15 Kenneth Wiedemann/E+/Getty Images; pp. 16–17, 18, 25 courtesy of the Library of Congress; p. 19 Zack Frank/Shutterstock.com; p. 28 AWL Images/Getty Images.

Printed in the United States of America

CPSIA compliance information: Batch #CS15GS: For further information contact Gareth Stevens, New York, New York at 1-800-542-2595.

CONTENTS

*Words in the glossary appear in **bold** type the first time they are used in the text.*

The ORIGINAL *Americans*

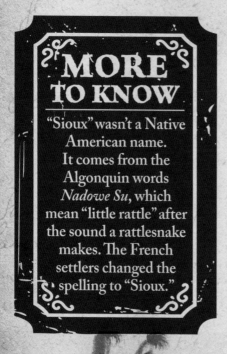

CHIEF SITTING BULL SIOUX -

Native Americans lived in North America for thousands of years before Europeans arrived. Different peoples had different **cultures**, histories, and religious beliefs. There were sometimes disagreements among them—even wars—but many groups cooperated and maintained peaceful relationships. However, once European explorers, traders, and settlers began pushing farther into

Sitting Bull's actual signature:

Native American territories, Native Americans faced difficult challenges to their ways of life, especially the loss of their lands.

Some individuals rose up to guide their people, lead battles, **negotiate** with the US government, and preserve traditions. Sitting Bull was a famous Sioux chief who thought coexistence with the *"white man"* was impossible. He said of the United States, *"This nation is like a spring **freshet**; it overruns its banks and destroys all who are in its path. We cannot dwell side by side."*

This Sioux camp may be similar to the one in which Sitting Bull grew up.

ORGANIZATION OF THE SIOUX

Native Americans were divided into independent groups, which were usually formed based on location. These were often made up of separate nations and were further broken down into tribes and bands. In the case of the Sioux, the Yankton, Teton, and Santee nations were spread across the Great Plains. Often, they were called by the language they spoke. Yankton spoke Nakota, Teton spoke Lakota, and the Santee spoke Dakota. Sitting Bull was of the Bad Bow band of the Hunkpapa tribe of the Lakota nation.

GROWING UP
Sioux

WHAT'S IN A NAME?

Sitting Bull's parents, Sitting Bull and Her Holy Door, named him Jumping Badger. As a child, he was given the nickname Hunkeshni, which meant "slow." It wasn't because he was always behind others or that he took a long time to do things. Instead, he was careful in choosing his words and actions and didn't make quick decisions. He was honored with his father's name, Sitting Bull, after proving himself on the battlefield.

Sitting Bull was born in the spring of 1831 in what is now South Dakota. Growing up, he was taught to ride horses and hunt, especially buffalo. Before each hunt, he would repeat to the animal, *"Grandfather, my children are hungry. You were created for that. So I must kill you."* By the age of 10, he had killed his first buffalo and shared it with tribe members who couldn't hunt, showing signs of the generous leader he would later become.

The Crow people, who also lived on the Plains, were the enemy of the Lakota at that time. Sitting Bull became a true warrior when, at 14 years old, he went to battle against the Crow for the first time.

MORE TO KNOW

The Lakota relied on the buffalo for everything: its meat was food, its hide provided clothing and shelter, its bones were made into tools and weapons, and its horns became jewelry. The Lakota word for buffalo was *tatanka*.

For a long time, the Sioux didn't use a written language to record their history or pass on traditions. They used symbols and drawings. This drawing shows a Lakota buffalo hunt.

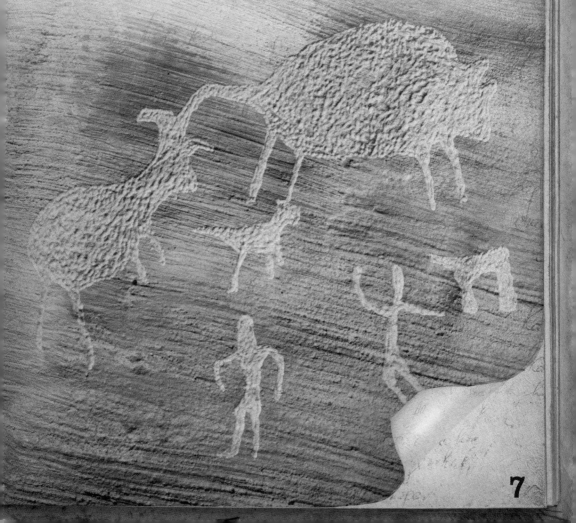

LEARNING TO
Distrust the White Man

In 1862, Dakota Sioux killed white settlers after US officials refused to give them food that had been promised in exchange for land. The Dakota were captured and hanged. However, the US military took action against other Sioux even though they hadn't been a part of the killings. Sitting Bull's first clash with the US military came in 1863. He would encounter them several more times over the next few years as the military invaded the Lakota hunting grounds.

MORE TO KNOW

The first treaty between Native Americans and the United States was written in 1778. Over the next 100 years, about 370 treaties were negotiated.

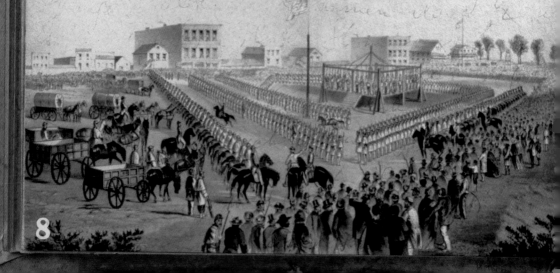

Sitting Bull thought the United States couldn't be trusted to honor treaties. He later said, *"We have now to deal with another people, small and feeble when our forefathers first met them, but now great and overbearing."* The Sioux were going to have to fight for all that was important to them.

The land the US government provided to the Sioux gradually shrank from a large territory in 1851 to smaller, separate reservations.

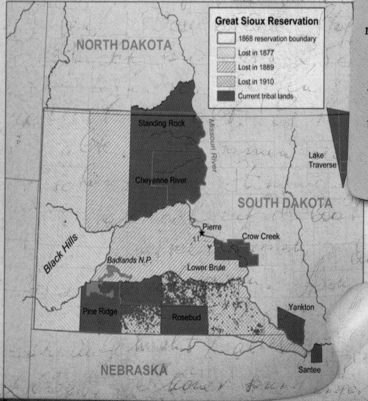

Great Sioux Reservation
☐ 1868 reservation boundary
☐ Lost in 1877
▨ Lost in 1889
▦ Lost in 1910
■ Current tribal lands

NORTH DAKOTA

Standing Rock

Missouri River

Lake Traverse

Cheyenne River

SOUTH DAKOTA

Black Hills

Pierre

Crow Creek

Badlands N.P.

Lower Brule

Pine Ridge

Rosebud

Yankton

NEBRASKA

Santee

DANGER TO PIONEERS?

The Fort Laramie Treaty of 1851 guaranteed wagon trains safe passage through Sioux territory on their way to the West Coast during the California gold rush (1848–1855). Native American nations also allowed roads and forts to be built in their territories in exchange for money that several tribes never received. Over 250,000 pioneers traveled through the territory, and fewer than 400 were killed.

A WARRIOR
Is Born

LAKOTA VALUES

The Lakota Sioux lived by several principles they considered to be important for their culture's survival. These included generosity *(wacantognaka)* of resources and time, courage *(woohitika)* to face difficulties, respect *(wowacintanka)* for all living things, wisdom *(woksape)* earned by experience and understanding of the world, and kinship *(wotitakuye)* or caring for other Lakota as family. A respected chief like Sitting Bull would have to demonstrate all these.

Sitting Bull and his people tried to carry on with their lives. He said, *"The farther my people keep away from the whites, the better I shall be satisfied."* However, increased wagon trains meant horses ate the grass buffalo needed to survive. White hunters used guns to kill large numbers of buffalo. These actions threatened the Lakota people's food source.

Sitting Bull's warriors weren't well matched against US soldiers. They mostly fought with bows and arrows. So, they used hit-and-run methods by attacking posts and leaving before the soldiers could counterattack.

Eventually, the Harney-Sanborn Treaty of 1865 set aside land for the Sioux, Arapaho, and Cheyenne nations. But when gold was discovered in Idaho and Montana, the government planned forts and permanent trails for **prospectors** in the territory they had promised to the Native Americans.

MORE TO KNOW

Sitting Bull belonged to the Midnight Strong Heart warrior society. He was one of two warriors who wore a band of cloth that was staked to the ground during battle. He would fight until his people won or he was killed.

The Bozeman Trail connected the Oregon Trail to the gold rush of Montana.

POLITICS,

Promises, and Problems

MORE TO KNOW

Sitting Bull walked with a limp much of his life. He was shot by a Crow chief, whom he killed.

Sitting Bull was elected a **principal** chief of the Sioux nation around 1867. In 1868, a new treaty—the Second Treaty of Fort Laramie—gave the Sioux a large reservation in what is now western South Dakota. This included the Black Hills. Many Lakota Sioux leaders signed the treaty, but Sitting Bull refused. He disapproved

that some Sioux were cooperating and becoming dependent on the government to feed them instead of keeping their hunting traditions.

Sitting Bull told the other chiefs, *"You are fools to make yourselves slaves to a piece of some fat bacon, some **hardtack**, and a little sugar and coffee."* Instead of moving to the reservation like the government expected them to, Sitting Bull and his followers continued to follow buffalo herds and disregard boundaries.

This photograph shows General William T. Sherman and other US officials meeting with Sioux to sign a peace treaty at Fort Laramie in 1868.

STANDING *Strong*

PRAISE FOR THE SIOUX

Though many white men saw Native Americans as savages, some respected their fighting and hunting skills and could appreciate their culture. Lieutenant James Gorrell, a British officer of the mid-1700s, called the Sioux *"certainly the greatest nation of Indians ever yet found. . . . They can shoot the wildest and largest beasts in the woods at seventy or one hundred yards distance. They are remarkable for their dancing; the other nations take their fashion from them."*

Two years after the 1868 treaty, gold was discovered in the Black Hills. Prospectors began entering Sioux territory, and the US government ordered the Sioux to allow them to do so. This was a **violation** of the treaty. The government tried to convince the Native Americans to retreat away from the Black Hills to a smaller portion of land. While other chiefs talked of asking for money, Sitting Bull believed the hills contained food and resources that couldn't be paid for. He described the Black Hills as *"a treasure to us Indians."* He further stated, *"If the whites try to take [the Black Hills], I will fight."*

The US government demanded all Indians move onto the reservation, so they could better control them. Those who didn't by January 31, 1876, would be considered hostile. Sitting Bull again refused.

Drawings like this one from 1860 convinced people that a fortune in gold was waiting to be claimed, even if it was on forbidden Sioux territory.

MORE TO KNOW

In 1872, during a battle with US soldiers, Sitting Bull teased the enemy by walking calmly into view, smoking a pipe, and then walking away. His nephew White Bull claimed it was *"the bravest deed possible."*

POWERS
of Prophecy

In spring 1876, about 8,000 Native Americans (mostly Sioux, Cheyenne, and Arapaho) ignored the government's orders and camped near Rosebud Creek in Montana Territory.

Sitting Bull said, *"We are an island of Indians in a lake of whites. We must stand together, or they will rub us out separately."*

In June 1876, Sitting Bull performed the traditional Sun Dance for 18 hours straight after being cut 50 times on each arm. He had a vision of soldiers falling headfirst into the Sioux camp. Sitting Bull thought this meant that his people would win a great victory. *"They want war. All right, we will give it to them,"* he said.

The Sioux and Cheyenne Indians at Rosebud Creek successfully pushed back US Army forces and their Indian **allies** on June 17, 1876.

Though a warrior, Sitting Bull was also known as a spiritual man. He had visions in which he communicated with animals, especially birds. He also believed he saw future events.

THE SUN DANCE

The Sun Dance was a 4-day religious event. Sometimes, holy men pierced the dancers' skin with bone and attached them to a pole or tree with ropes of animal hide. Dancers sometimes dragged heavy buffalo skulls behind them and had their skin sliced many times, like Sitting Bull experienced. The goal was to endure pain as they danced while trying to tear themselves free. They believed they would receive power, blessings, or understanding from spirit persons.

A MOMENTOUS
Clash

A SEEKER OF WISDOM

Sitting Bull believed himself to be a *wichasa wakan* (holy man). He once said: *"I was still in my mother's insides when I began to study all about my people. God . . . gave me the power to see out of the womb. I studied there, in the womb, about many things. . . . The God Almighty must have told me at that time . . . that I would be the man to be the judge of all the other Indians—a big man, to decide for them in all their ways."*

On June 25, 1876, Crow scouts reported to Lieutenant Colonel George Armstrong Custer that Sioux and Cheyenne Indians had relocated to Little Bighorn River. Rather than let them move camp again, Custer decided to attack. Gall, Sitting Bull's adopted brother and a chief, described the scene: *"The women and children were hastily moved downstream . . . [They] caught the horses for the bucks [warriors] to mount them; the bucks mounted and charged back."*

an artist's idea of the Indian warriors at the Battle of the Little Bighorn

18

Still recovering from his Sun Dance, Sitting Bull stayed back from the conflict to protect the camp and provide leadership.

Custer and 210 of his men were killed in just 1 hour. Sitting Bull later recalled, *"They were brave men, but they were too tired. When they rode up, their horses were tired and they were tired."* He felt his Sun Dance vision had come true.

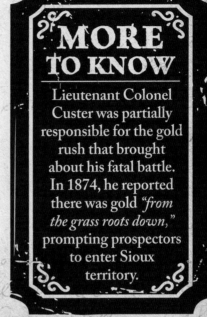

MORE TO KNOW

Lieutenant Colonel Custer was partially responsible for the gold rush that brought about his fatal battle. In 1874, he reported there was gold *"from the grass roots down,"* prompting prospectors to enter Sioux territory.

These headstones mark the graves of cavalry soldiers who died during the Battle of the Little Bighorn.

ESCAPE
to Canada

Many chiefs knew the government would **retaliate** for the Battle of the Little Bighorn, but Sitting Bull refused to surrender. He led about 3,000 Sioux across the Canadian border in spring 1877, hoping to find **refuge** in a new country. The Canadian government welcomed them to stay as long as they were peaceful.

MORE TO KNOW

Not all Sioux chiefs agreed what was best for their people. Red Cloud of the Oglalas and Spotted Tail of the Brules thought that accepting life on a reservation was the best chance for survival.

Heading north into Canada meant harsher winters. This painting shows Sioux hunting buffalo in the snow.

US officials tried to convince him to return. His people could exchange their weapons and horses for cows to farm. But Sitting Bull told them, *"For sixty-four years you have kept me and my people, and treated us bad. . . . If you think I am a fool, you are a bigger fool than I am. . . . You come here to tell us lies, but we don't want to hear them. . . . I intend to stay here."*

Sitting Bull

CANADIAN NATIVES

Native Americans lived in Canada before Europeans came. However, there wasn't as much conflict between these tribes and the Canadian government and citizens as within the United States. The US population grew more rapidly and spread west much faster and with less regulation. The Canadians moved into new territory gradually and with more governmental control. The Canadians relied on their well-trained North West Mounted Police, or Mounties, to keep order and interpret the law.

A HARD *Decision*

The Sioux struggled to survive in Canada for 4 years. The buffalo there were disappearing from overhunting, as they had been in the United States, and the Canadian government wouldn't supply food. US captain Walter Clifford described Sitting Bull's choice: *"Nothing but nakedness and starvation had driven this man to submission and that not on his own account but for the sake of his children."*

On July 19, 1881, Sitting Bull traveled to Fort Buford in Montana and had his son hand Sitting Bull's gun over to the officials. The Lakota chief said, *"I surrender this rifle to you through my* young son, whom I now desire to teach in this manner that he has become a friend of the whites . . . I wish to be remembered as the last man of my tribe to give up my rifle."

Many Sioux returned to the United States before Sitting Bull. This illustration shows Sioux under Chief Gall returning to the United States from Canada.

ADAPTING
to a New Life

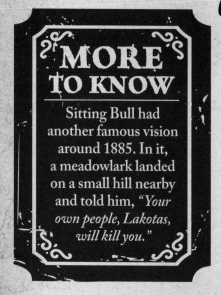
Because the US government was afraid Sitting Bull would start an uprising at a reservation, he was imprisoned for almost 2 years at Fort Randall in South Dakota. In 1883, he was finally allowed to rejoin his people at Standing Rock Reservation. However, the General Allotment Act, or Dawes Act, of 1889 divided the Sioux Reservation into five smaller reservations. Native American families received individual plots of land to farm.

Sitting Bull spoke against the government planning their lives: *"This land belongs to us, for the Great Spirit gave it to us when he put us here. We were free to come and go, and to live in our own way. But white men, who belong to another land, have come upon us, and are forcing us to live according to their ideas. This is an injustice; we have never dreamed of making white men live as we live."*

Sitting Bull poses with Buffalo Bill Cody.

WILD WEST SHOW

William "Buffalo Bill" Cody was a former US army soldier and scout. When his famous Wild West show toured, he added well-known people as performers to increase ticket sales. In 1885, Sitting Bull joined the show for a few months. Despite often facing boos and taunts from audiences who thought of him as a savage, he drew large crowds and became friends with the famous sharpshooter Annie Oakley.

THE END
of a Journey

A belief was spreading among the reservations that a ceremony called the Ghost Dance could restore the Native Americans' way of life. Government officials began to worry the Sioux would rise up against them. They decided to arrest Sitting Bull, so he couldn't lead a rebellion.

On December 15, 1890, 43 Lakota policemen surrounded his cabin and ordered him outside. His supporters and the police began arguing. Sitting Bull was shot twice, once in the back of the head, and quickly died. Sitting Bull once said, *"First kill me, before you can take possession of my fatherland!"* That statement had become reality.

The great chief was buried at Fort Yates in North Dakota, but his people wanted him to rest in his homeland. In 1953, his remains were reburied in Mobridge, South Dakota.

MORE TO KNOW

The men who shot Sitting Bull were Lakota men acting as policemen. Sitting Bull's earlier vision that Lakota would kill him came true.

This photo was taken in 1884, about 6 years before Sitting Bull died.

A LEGACY
of Respect

During Sitting Bull's lifetime, the Lakota Sioux went from free-roaming, buffalo-hunting, powerful warriors to a nation confined to reservations and forced to adopt another culture. Cheyenne warrior Wooden Leg described the respect many had for the chief: *"I am not ashamed to tell I was a follower of Sitting Bull. . . . He had a big brain and a good one, a strong heart and a generous one."*

Through battles, negotiations, and hardships, Sitting Bull always felt destined to lead: *"The place I hold among my people was held by my ancestors before me . . . I am satisfied that I was brought into this life for a purpose."* His purpose was leadership. Today, people of many backgrounds and cultures admire him for it.

Many Lakota continue traditions and honor their tribe's history while living on reservations.

TIMELINE
THE LIFE OF SITTING BULL

Sitting Bull born in what is now South Dakota — **about 1831**

about 1845 — Sitting Bull battles against Crow for first time

Sitting Bull's first clash with US military — **1863**

1865 — Harney-Sanborn Treaty gives lands to Sioux, Arapaho, and Cheyenne nations

Sitting Bull elected chief of Sioux nation — **1867**

1868 — Second Treaty of Fort Laramie gives Sioux land in what is now western South Dakota

Sitting Bull performs Sun Dance — **1876**

1876 — Battle of the Little Bighorn results in defeat of US military on June 25

Sitting Bull leads Sioux into Canada — **1877**

1881 — Sitting Bull surrenders in Montana on July 19

Sitting Bull allowed to live on Standing Rock Reservation — **1883**

1885 — Sitting Bull joins Buffalo Bill's Wild West show

Dawes Act divides Sioux reservation into five smaller reservations — **1889**

1890 — Sitting Bull killed by Lakota police

BATTLE OF WOUNDED KNEE

After Sitting Bull's death, soldiers followed a band of Sioux to Wounded Knee Creek. The Sioux were ordered to surrender their weapons, but a struggle over a rifle began an unevenly matched confrontation that left nearly 300 Sioux dead. Black Elk later said, *"I can still see the butchered women and children lying heaped and scattered . . . A people's dream died there."* It was the last major military conflict between the United States and Native Americans.

29

GLOSSARY

ally: one of two or more people or groups who work together

culture: the beliefs and ways of life of a group of people

freshet: an overflowing of a stream caused by heavy rains or melting snow

hardtack: a saltless hard bread

negotiate: to come to an agreement

principal: among the first in importance or rank

prospector: someone who searches an area for valued resources, such as gold

refuge: a place set aside for people to live safely

reservation: land set aside by the US government for Native Americans

retaliate: to harm somebody in response or revenge for a harm done

unconscious: unable to see, hear, or sense what is happening because of accident or injury, as if asleep

violation: the act of ignoring someone's rights. Also, the act of breaking a law.

womb: the part of a woman's body in which a baby grows

FOR MORE
Information

Books

Jeffrey, Gary, and Kate Petty. *Sitting Bull: The Life of a Lakota Sioux Chief.* New York, NY: Rosen Publishing Group, 2005.

Sanford, William R. *Hunkpapa Lakota Chief Sitting Bull.* Berkeley Heights, NJ: Enslow Publishers, 2013.

Stanley, George E. *Sitting Bull: Great Sioux Hero.* New York, NY: Sterling Publishing, 2010.

Websites

Lakota Indian Fact Sheet
www.bigorrin.org/lakota_kids.htm
Explore the history, culture, and modern way of life of Sitting Bull's Lakota nation through a variety of informative links.

Little Bighorn Battlefield National Monument
www.nps.gov/libi/index.htm
Learn about Sitting Bull's most famous conflict through maps, photos, and a summary of the battle.

Sitting Bull
www.pbs.org/weta/thewest/people/s_z/sittingbull.htm
Read a biography of Sitting Bull.

INDEX